WHY BLACK MEN CHOOSE WHITE WOMEN

By Dr. Rosie Milligan

Published By
Milligan Books

Cover Design
By Tony Quaid

Formatting By
AbarCo Business Services

Dr. Rosie Milligan

Published and Distributed by:
Milligan Books
an imprint of Professional Business Consultants
1425 W. Manchester, Suite B,
Los Angeles, California 90047
(213) 750-3592

First Printing, August 1998
10 9 8 7 6 5 4 3 2

ISBN 1- 881524-19-1

Table of Contents

Table of Contents

Personal Acknowledgments

I am truly thankful to Barbara Lindsey for pushing me into a journey of writing books. She pushed me to the finishing line with all eight books. Barbara, I truly thank you.

To Ruby Smith, who has said, "Girl, I see greatness in you." Thank you for believing in me.

To my sister-friend and business partner, Mary Lee Crump, who has always made "such-a-to-do" out of everything that I have ever done. I thank you for being there for me, emotionally and financially. You helped me to realize my dreams.

I acknowledge my loving children, Pamela Milligan McGee, M.D., John Milligan, Jr., my cosmetologist; my son-in-law, Elder Kelvin McGee; Cedric Milligan, my assistant business manager; my godson William Streeter and his lovely wife, Evette Streeter; my goddaughter, Dorotha Steed, and my godson, Delano Cagnalotti.

I also acknowledge my sisters and brothers who have considered me their mentor; mother-sister Owen Nelson, Margaret Hoskins, Willie McCue, Kenyaka Mamahi, Dianne Jerald, Pera Jones, Virginia Walton, And Clara King who has shared all of my woes throughout my childhood and adult life; and my brothers Leroy Hunter and Robert Hunter.

To my godfather, Rev. Louis Jones, thank you for your support and encouragement.

To Oneida and Oliver Tolbert, and to my many friends who helped, I cannot name you all, you know who you are, I do love, appreciate, and thank you.

Biography

Dr. Rosie Milligan

Dr. Rosie Milligan, registered nurse, counselor/ health consultant, author, and Ph.D. in Business Administration, has been an achiever most of her life. She has always been involved in a career or business in which she was helping other people accomplish what they wanted in life. Her motto, "Erase 'No'-Step Over 'Can't' and Move Forward With Life," has been a motivating influence to hundreds to whom she has been mentor and role model.

The mother of three entrepreneurs-an M.D., a cosmetologist, a health food store owner - Dr. Milligan lectures nationally on economic empowerment, managing diversity in the workplace, and male-female relationships. Her books, **Satisfying The Black Man/ Woman Sexually Made Simple'**, and **'Nigger, Please,'** raised eyebrows across the country.

As an economic empowerment activist, the Mississippi native owns a publishing company, a book store, Cinell hair care products, and Professional Business Consulting Services. A successful motivational speaker and trainer, she has appeared on numerous television and radio shows, such as; Sally Jesse Raphael, in New York; People Are Talking, in San Francisco; Maury Povich, in New York; A.M. Philadelphia; Evening Exchange, in Washington, D. C.;

Marilyn Kagan, in Los Angeles, and she's a regular guest on Stevie Wonder's KJLH Radio. Dr. Milligan co-hosts the Financial Freedom Forum on cable television. She is founder and director of Black Writers on Tour.

The author of eight books and co-author of two, Dr. Milligan releases her newest book, **"Why Black Men Choose White Women"**.

Preface

As Blacks strive to enhance their socio-economic status, their educational status, their political status, little emphasis is placed on building Black male/female Relationships. When the matter is discussed, it is on a superficial level. Most Black male/female dialogue consists of pointing fingers and casting blame. Healing can only take place between Black men and women when we stop blaming and start accepting each other, and seeing our behavior as the products of slavery as adaptations to a hostile environment. All that the Black man and Black woman is, he/she was conditioned to be. Dr. Frances Cress Welsign in The Isis Paper states:

> *"For all that we can imagine doing and all that we will do or fail to do is a result of that picture of `self,' derived from our total experiences from birth onward. That picture becomes the basis for all our behavioral patterns. Unfortunately, a major part of these self and group images for all too many of us Blacks consists of a brief and inaccurate history."*

The Black man and Black woman are in need of a slavery debriefing. Our struggle for liberation is both internal and external. At this point in our history, statistics prove we are more destructive to ourselves then any external force is to us. The symptoms that Blacks manifest are the result of being an oppressed people: low self-esteem, self-hatred, the love and envy of and the desire to emulate the oppressor.

INTRODUCTION

Why Black men choose White women is a question that is long overdue for an answer. I have been researching the answer to this million-dollar question for eight years. After years of research and survey, I have found the answer. At first I was afraid to reveal my findings. I knew how badly I would be attacked by both Black men and Black women.

Black men would argue that all Black men do not want White women. They would accuse me of insulting their intellect and their Black manhood. I agree that all Black men do not want a White woman; however, most Black men will disregard this statement. They will accuse me of saying to the White people, that all Brothers want White women.

Black women would accuse me of making excuses for Black men who neglect them for White women. They will accuse me of blaming them for the decisions made by Black men to choose White women. Black women will allege that I am insensitive to their hurt and pain.

Black folks take issue with another Black person who tells the truth about Blacks in public. They call it 'airing dirty linen'. Blacks also take issue with Blacks who do not agree with the Black Majority opinion. Somehow there is a notion that when in public, Blacks must show a united front. I do not have to tell non-Blacks that we are divided on most issues. The proof is in the pudding. I do not have to tell non-Blacks that most Black folks have a preference for non-Blacks and particularly for Whites. The proof is in the pudding. Who do Blacks do business with? What does this question have to do with Black male/female relationships? Let's examine the psychology of Blacks relating to Whites.

You must consider the residual effects on the psyche of being raised in a nation where your ancestors were slaves and therefore not considered human. And living in a country which still has vestiges of that same calculated system of human mind enslavement and denigration, we have gone through several name changes. Yes, we say it loud that we are Black and we are proud. Yet, Black women continue to emulate the white look as much as possible. Blacks continue to refer to little Black girls as beautiful when they have light complexions and straight hair (good hair as we call it).

Recently, on national television, when little Black girls were asked to select a doll, they chose a white doll. They said that the black doll was ugly and the white doll was pretty.

Men are more likely than women to choose their mates on the basis of physical attraction. Conversely, Black men, many of whom have internalized the same European conception of physical attractiveness, are more likely to find White women who meet their criteria. In spite of the racial problem in America, the number of Black men who are seeking White women will increase. One reason is that Blacks, and Black children in particular, watch more television than any other ethnic group. Television is a powerful tool that conveys a subconscious message that white is good and black is bad. The media, including some Black Rap Music, help spread the idea that a White woman is 'The Woman.'

CHAPTER 1

A Close-Up Look At Black
Male/Female Relationships

CHAPTER 1

A Close-Up Look At
Black Male/Female Relationships

The first and foremost order of business is that the Black man/woman must understand that they are not Caucasian clones. Sidney Winfield, in his book <u>Positive African American Men-United</u>, had the following to say:

> *Only African-American men can define the standard by which they are judged as men. We have not created a culture or society based on princi-*

ples which work for us. Black male/
female relationships will never get
better, as long as they are being judged
by the standards of their oppressors."

The following is a quote by Victoria King in her book, <u>Manhandled</u>. Victoria King expresses a similar sentiment:

Of course you will say, "How can I love
and want to be with you when I come
home and you're like a slob. Why White
women never open the door for their
husbands the way you Black bitches do."
I should guess not, you ignorant man.
Why should they be in such a state when
they've got maids like me to do every-
thing for them? There is no screaming
at the kids for her; no standing over the
hot stove; everything is done for her, and
whether her man loves her or not, he
provides . . . . do you hear that, Nigger?
PROVIDES!

I guess you are wondering, what does all this have to do with Black men choosing White women? Read on!

The average Black male/female born in America is hostile, bitter, angry, financially deprived, heart-broken, insecure, non-trusting, and fearful. So what happens when you put two explosives together? The average Black man/woman is overly sensitive, easily hurt, very defensive, and does not accept criticism well. There are justifiable reasons for their behavior; however, the reasons do not help heal Black families.

The Black man and Black woman are in a tug-of-war. Therefore, for sanity's sake, some Black men will choose the path of least resistance. Don't get mad; keep reading and get educated. The following is an excerpt from my book, <u>Satisfying The Black Man Sexually Made Simple</u>, a companion book to, <u>Satisfying The Black Woman Sexually Made Simple</u>:

> *Many Black men are not as assertive*
> *and aggressive as his mate would*
> *want him to be. The Black man has*
> *difficulties in those areas because he*

has been socialized to take the back seat and to demonstrate a low profile when dealing with the female. The Black male environment, for the most part, consisted of the female gender. The Black man comes from a home most often dominated by females, a school dominated by females. Usually a younger sister was left in charge to dominate the older male child while his mother was away. The church was the only place, many times, where the Black male observed men in charge. May be that is the reason why we have so many Black preachers and Black churches, for the church is the only institution in which Black men have been given freedom to dominate, have power over and control. The Black man is expected to assume a role that he has not been prepared for in most cases. The focus and attention now given to the Black male child today will certainly change and improve the future course for the Black man.

If there is any truth to the stereotype that White women are easy-going, then it's understandable why Black men would rather switch than fight. If Blacks would examine each other as *Black* males, and *Black* females, not just as males and females, they would view each other in a more positive way.

We have not corrected our problems, because we are made to feel guilty when we look back. Yes, our oppressor caused many of our problems, but we must find our solution. And only the whole truth will set us free.

In order to move forward in a positive and healthy manner, we must begin our debriefing. If we do not understand white supremacist and its institutionalized affects on Black people all over the world, then all I have said to you, and all I will ever say to you, will not make a difference in your quest for a better life and a better relationship between Black males and females.

The debriefing process must begin with understanding the following excerpts from my book, <u>Nigger Please</u>. It would serve you well to read the entire book. Let Us Make a Slave and the <u>Willie Lynch Letter</u> are quoted from <u>Back Door to Racism</u>, by Kamal Karriem. Willie Lynch was a slave owner in the West Indies, who used mind control techniques on his Black slaves, and he described his techniques for other slave owners:

LET US MAKE A SLAVE

Let us make a slave. What do we need? First of all we need a black nigger man, a pregnant nigger woman and her baby nigger boy. Second, we will use the same basic principle that we use in breaking a horse, combined with some more sustaining factors. What we do with horses is that we break them from one form of life to another, that is, we reduce them from their natural state in nature; where-as nature provides them with the natural capacity to take care of their needs and the needs of their offspring, we break that natural sting of independence from them and thereby create a dependency state so that we may be able to get from them useful production for our business and pleasure.

CARDINAL PRINCIPLES FOR MAKING A NEGRO

For fear that our future generations may not understand the principles of breaking both horses and men, we lay down the art. For, if we are to sustain our basic economy and comprehensive economic planning: we must break and tie both of the beasts together, the nigger and the horse. We understand that short range planning in economics results in periodic economic chaos; so that to avoid turmoil in the economy, it requires us to have breadth and depth in long range comprehensive planning, articulating both skill and sharp perception.

We lay down the following principles

for long range comprehensive economic planning:

1. Both horse and nigger are no good to economy in the wild or natural state.

2. Both must be broken and tied together for orderly production.

3. For orderly futures, special and particular attention must be paid to the females and the young offspring.

4. Both must be crossbred to produce a variety and division of labor.

5. Both must be taught to respond to a peculiar new language.

6. Psychological and physical institutions of containment must be created for both.

We hold the above six cardinal principles as truths to be self-evident, based on the following discourse concerning the economics of breaking and tying the horse and nigger together – all inclusive of the six principles laid down above.

NOTE: Neither principle alone will suffice for good economics. All principles must be employed for the orderly good of the nation.

Accordingly, both a wild horse and a wild or natural nigger is dangerous even if captured, for they will have the tendency to seek their customary freedom, and, in doing so, might kill you in your sleep. You cannot rest. They sleep while you are awake, and are awake while you sleep. They are dangerous near the family house, and it requires too much labor to watch them away from the house Above all, you cannot get them to work in this natural state.

Hence, both the horse and the nigger must be broken; that is, break them from one form of mental life to another – keep the body and take the mind. In other words, break the will to resist. Now the breaking process is the same for both the horse and the nigger, only slightly varying in degrees. But as we said before, there is an art in long range economic planning. You must keep your eye and thoughts on the female and the offspring of the horse and the nigger.

A brief discourse in offspring development will shed light on the key to sound economic principles. Pay little attention to the generation of original breaking but concentrate on future generation. Therefore, if you break the female mother, she will break the offspring in its early years of development and, when the offspring is old enough to work, she will deliver it up to you for their normal female protective tendencies will have been lost in the original breaking process.

For example, take the case of the wild stud horse, a female horse and an already infant horse and compare the breaking process with two captured nigger males in the natural state, a pregnant nigger woman with her infant offspring. Take the stud horse, break him for limited containment. Completely break the female horse until she becomes very gentle where you or anybody can ride her in comfort. Breed the mare and the stud until you have desired offspring. Then you can turn the stud to freedom until you need him again. Train the female horse whereby she will eat out of your hand, and she will, in turn, train the infant horse to eat out of your hand also.

When it comes to breaking the uncivilized niggers, use the same process, but vary the degrees and step up the pressure so as to do a complete reversal of the mind. Take the meanest and most restless nigger, strip him of his clothes in front of the remaining male niggers, the female, and the nigger infant, tar and feather him, tie each leg to a different horse faced in opposite directions, set him afire and beat both horses to pull him apart in front of the remaining nigger. The next step is to take a bull-whip and beat the remaining nigger male to the point of death in front of the female and the infant. Don't kill him, but put the fear of God in him, for he can be useful for future breeding.

THE BREAKING PROCESS OF THE WOMAN

Then take the female. Run a series of tests on her to see if she will submit to your desires willingly. TEST her in every.... way because she is the most important factor for good economics. If she shows any sign of resistance in submitting completely to your will, do not hesitate to use the bullwhip on her to extract the last bit of bitch out of her. Take care not to kill her, for, in doing so, you spoil good economics. When in complete submission, she will train her offspring in the early years to submit to labor when they become of age.

Understanding is the best thing. Therefore, we shall go deeper into this area of the subject matter concerning what we have produced here in this breaking process of the nigger. We have reversed the relationships. In her natural uncivilized state she would have a strong dependency on the uncivilized nigger male, and she would have a limited protective tendency toward her independent male offspring and would raise the female offspring to be dependent like her. Nature had provided for this type of balance. We reversed nature by burning and pulling one uncivilized nigger apart and bull whipping the other to the point of death- all in her presence.

*By her being left alone, unprotected, with the **male image destroyed**, the ordeal causes...... her to move from her psychological dependent state to a **frozen independent state**. In this frozen psychological state of independence, she will raise her male and female offspring in reverse roles.*

*For fear of the **young male's life**,
she psychologically train him to be
mentally weak and **dependent but
physically strong**. Because she has
become psychologically independent,
she will train her female offspring to
be **psychologically independent----**.
What you got? You've got a nigger
woman out front and the nigger man
behind and scared. This is a perfect
situation for **sound sleep** and **good
economics**.*

THE NEGRO MARRIAGE UNIT

*We breed two nigger males with two
nigger females. Then we take the
nigger males away from them and
keep them moving and working. Say
the one nigger female bears a nigger
female and the other bears a nigger
male. Both nigger females, being
without influence of the nigger male
image, frozen with an independent
psychology, will raise their offspring
into reversed positions. The one with
the female offspring will teach her to*

*be like herself, **independent** and ne-gotiable (we negotiate with her, through her, by her, and negotiate her at will). The one with the nigger male off-spring, she being **frozen with a sub-conscious fear** for his life, will raise him to be mentally dependent and weak, but **physically** strong — in other words, **body over mind.** Now, in a few years when these two off-spring become fertile for early re-production, we will mate and breed them and continue the cycle. That is good, sound, and long range com-prehensive planning.*

WILLIE LYNCH LETTER
TO
SLAVE MASTERS

Gentlemen: I greet you here on the bank of the James River in the year of Our Lord one thousand seven hund-red and twelve. First, I shall thank you The Gentlemen of the Colony of Virginia for bringing me here. I am here to help you solve some of you problems with slaves. Your invitation reached me on my modest plantation in the West Indies where I have experimented with some of the newest and still oldest methods for control of slaves. Ancient Rome would envy us if my program is implemented. As our boat sailed south on the James River, named for our illustrious King, whose version of the Bible we cherish, I saw enough to know that your problem is not unique. While Rome used cords of wood as crosses for standing human bodies along its old highways in great numbers, you are here using the tree and rope on occasion.

I caught the whiff of a dead slave hanging from a tree a couple miles back. You are not only losing valuable stock by hanging, you are having uprisings, slaves are running away, your crops are sometimes left in the field too long for maximum profit, you suffer occasional fires, your animals are killed, gentlemen, you know what your problems are; I do not need to elaborate. I am not here to enumerate your problems; I am here to introduce you to a method of solving them.

In my bag here, I have a foolproof method for controlling Black Slaves. I guarantee every one of you that if installed correctly, it will control the slaves for at least 300 years. My method is simple and members of your family and only Overseer can use it.

I have outlines a number of difference(s) among the slaves; and I take these differences and make them bigger. I use fear, distrust, and envy for control purposes. These methods have worked on my modest plantation in the West Indies and [they] will work throughout the South. Take this simple little list of differences, think about them. On top of my list is "Age" but it is there only because it begins with an "a." or The second is "Color" "Shade," there is intelligence, size, sex, size of

plantation, status of plantation, atti-
tude of owner, whether the slaves live
in the valley, on a hill, East, West,
North, or South, have fine or coarse
hair, or is tall or short.   Now that
you have a list of differences, I shall
give you an outline of action, but
before that, I shall assure you that
distrust is stronger than trust and
envy is stronger than adulation, re-
spect and admiration.

The Black Slave, after receiving this
indoctrination, shall carry on and will
become self - refueling and self - gener-
ating for hundreds of years, maybe
thousands.

Don't forget you must pitch the old
black versus the young black and the
young black male against the old black
male.   You must use the dark skin
slaves vs. the light skin slaves and
the light skin slaves vs. the dark skin
slaves. You must also have your white ser-
vants and overseers distrust all blacks,
but it is necessary that your slaves

34

trust and depend on us.

Gentlemen, these Kits are keys to control, use them. Have your wives and children use them, never miss an opportunity. My plan is guaranteed and the good thing about this plan is that if used intensely for one year the slaves themselves will remain perpetually distrustful.

Thank you gentlemen.

Hopefully, this chapter's conclusion will motivate Blacks to re-examine themselves, and will provoke non-blacks to embrace the Black male/female from a new perspective. It is time to get up, shake off the dirt and rise to a higher level.

We are not suffering from lack of motivation; we suffer a lack of self-appreciation and self-knowledge. Our self-esteem must be enhanced. We must examine our past strengths and achievements, and reach a better understanding of how we arrived in this condition in the first place. It is easier to figure out how to get out of a situation if you know how you got into it. That's logical, isn't it?

Self-esteem breeds self-love, self-worth, and self-pride. One can only be capable of loving others after learning to love oneself. One can only appreciate others after learning to appreciate oneself. Our behavior is a reflection of how we see ourselves.

The Real Truth About
Black Women And Sex

CHAPTER 2

The Real Truth About Black Women And Sex

We must examine the Black woman as we discuss why Black men choose White women. Black men do not have a standard to measure the African American women other than by the European standards. A Black woman's sexual experiences, the social setting in which she was reared, her physical capabilities, religious background, and upbringing all have a strong impact and influence on how she genuinely feels about sex; how much she enjoys sex; and her willingness to explore various positions and exotic practices during sex. The Black woman's history will be expounded on in later chapters, so that you will have a better insight into the present nature of the Black woman, and how her nature reflects her past. To understand the present condition of any sex or race, the past condition or history must be examined and understood. If a Black woman has a personal history or family history of rape, she will certainly not enjoy any act that makes her feel helpless, controlled, or violated, like the whip and chain approach when the woman is slapped, scratched, or abused on any parts of her body.

The Black woman does not like to be called names such as bitch or whore while making love. She does not find such sexual practices to be romantic or sexually fulfilling. All men must realize that the Black woman has a unique perspective. She has a background and history of her own that is far different from those of women from other ethnic groups. Nevertheless, there are also differences among Black women in their likes and dislikes about sex, and these things should be communicated between sexual partners.

While some Black women may have no sexual limitations or inhibitions, other Black women may find certain requests their lovers make to be demeaning and degrading. Black women do not embrace their sexually as freely and honestly as other women. This is due to her being made to feel ashamed of her body and due to her history of rape at a very early age, and of being forced to abandon her babies. Prior to the drug epidemic, Black women were the least likely women to separate willingly from their babies.

Many white men had their very first (and best) sexual encounters with a Black woman, so that they could keep their own women pure and unspoiled until marriage. They raped the young black female, usually by the age of thirteen. The

White men found much pleasure in having sex with the Black woman. He acquired an addiction for her body, even after entering into marriage, he continued to sneak out of his house in the late hours of the night to find pleasure by having sex with the Black Woman.

Whenever the White man was caught in the act of raping a Black woman, the Black woman was severely beaten by the White woman. White women were most cruel towards the Black Women during slavery because she envied the body that the White man lusted for day and night. When the Black Woman gave birth to a light-skinned baby, the White women knew that some White woman's husband was the father. The White woman always tried to make the Black woman feel ugly, less than a woman, and less then a human being.

Some Black women today are still ashamed of their bodies if they have a few extra pounds here and there, especially, if they are well endowed in the hip, thigh, and breast areas. The Black woman is a very shapely, sensuous woman. She is often so obsessed with the European standard of beauty of five feet six, size six dress, size seven shoe, waist of 22 inches, small breasts, thin lips, green or blue eyes, etc., that she sometimes forgets the unique beauty of the African woman. The Black woman's perfect breasts, broad hips, and her beautiful thick lips, are envied all around the world.

As a result of slavery, many Black women today have not learned to appreciate their physical differences, and therefore, have not learned to express their sexuality fully. Many Black women spend countless hours trying to work off their cushion (healthy buttocks). They do not realize that men are experiencing much pleasure as a result of her well endowed behind (cushion).

Picture a typical Black woman lying in bed

on her back. Visualize her body, her round well-endowed behind, places her body in an exciting position. Visualize her body lying on her side. Visualize her body standing in an erect position. The Black woman's body is sensuous from any angle East, West, North, and South. Now picture a woman with a flat behind lying in bed in the same position. Men find themselves having to place their hands under her buttocks to elevate her to the right position a position that is natural for a typical Black woman.

A man making love to a woman with well-endowed buttocks can find other uses for his hands to bring about even more pleasure. Most Black women are not aware that they have been blessed with a built in comfortable rocking chair (cushion).

Today as we approach the new millennium, one hundred and thirty-three years post Emancipation Proclamation, Black girls and

Black women are the most frequent victims of rape and assault. Is the oppressor raping the Black girl and the Black woman? She is mentally raped by the oppressor and physically raped by Black boys and Black men. Sexual abuse is so prevalent amount young Black girls. There is a high incidence of chemically dependent mothers encouraging and initiating sexual activities between men and their daughters for drug money. There are too many Blacks living under the illusion that Blacks do not commit such sexual crimes against children. Therefore, Black girls and boys are left unprotected, and placed in situations where they are victims of sexual abuse on a daily basis.

According to Sidney Winfield, a certified master social worker:

> *"One of the greatest unspoken problems our women face is the sexual abuse suffered as young girls. It appears countless numbers of young*

<u>women from 9-18 are abused sexu-</u>
<u>ally by young boys, young men, and</u>
<u>men</u>. Most of these attacks go unre-
ported but leave deep psychological,
emotional, and spiritual scars on our
girls. The strong who learned how to
physically fight, like a man, and defend
themselves, escape sexual penetration.
The average and the weak are vic-
timized. At this time, there is no way
to know how many adult women carry
secrets of rape and physical attack. It
is unknown how many children have
been born resulting from a forced sex-
ual act. There can be no peace, posi-
tive communication, or unity among
our people until these atrocities cease.
Many of the problems couples experi-
ence are the result of these unspoken
and untreated incidents. Many of the
negative attitudes held by our women
are a result of legitimate grievances
against male beast-like treatment."

I hear you asking, what does all this have
to do with Black men choosing White women?
Let me explain. Girls and women who are

victims of physical and sexual abuse have difficulty in the areas of sensuality and sexuality. Many of these victims have difficulty with intimacy. There is much paranoia among Black women today. They witness their mothers, sisters and friends being left alone after becoming pregnant to shoulder the full responsibility as caretaker for their children.

Black females continue to search for love. In their quest for love, they get sex and a baby. During my many years of research, I've discovered that there are many Black women who are sexually impotent. These women have no desire to have sexual intercourse. They do have sex with men as a prerequisite to building a relationship in hopes that it could lead to a marriage union. In many cases, their sexual problems begin the night of the honeymoon. The husband is feeling inadequate as a male. He becomes frustrated and sometimes abusive. The truth is, there is nothing wrong with him sexually. He is dealing with an impotent woman, one who has suffered sexual abuse or who has witnessed it. She is afraid to tell him that she has no love nor desire for sex; she loves only the social aspect of the marriage.

Is sex important to a Black man? Sex is the only form of gratification within reach for the economically deprived man. He cannot take a weekend cruise. He cannot hide away in his yacht at sea. He finds himself trying to crawl back into the uterus (womb) for comfort via the warm vagina. The vagina becomes the hideout for Black men seeking to escape the woes of life's challenges.

Sex is one of the most sought-after experiences. Besides money, sex is the only factor in our civilized societies that people pursue at the risk of causing harm to themselves. Men have lost their jobs for it; men have lost their lives for it; have gone AWOL from the military for it; and all for a few short hours of pleasure and a few seconds of orgasmic thrills.

Does being a product of slavery, and having a history of rape and sexual abuse, correlate in any way with sexual freedom and sex inhibitions? Let us examine a comparison of the sexuality of Whites, African Americans, Latinos, and Asian Americans. This comparison was obtained from a college textbook, Understanding Human Sexuality. Shirley Hyde/ John Delanmater.

Whites-African-Americans-Latinos – Asians American

Percent who mastur-bated in the last year	White	Black	Hispanic	Asian
Men	67%	40%	67%	61%
Women	44%	32%	35%	NA
Percent who have performed oral sex				
Men	81%	51%	71%	64%
Women	75%	34%	60%	NA
Percent of 30 to 34 years old who have never been married				
Men	25%	45%	25%	NA
Women	14%	35%	17%	NA

Black women want to be loved, not sexed. Black women want their Black men to come home, and help them formulate a definition of Black man and Black woman that works for them. The Black man needs sex as a mean of determining his self-worth, and the Black woman is afraid of it. This makes communication difficult between the Black male and female on sexual issues.

All women have somethings in common, however, the Black woman is the most frequent woman to be left alone to rear the offsprings from her sexual experience. Therefore, sex for any Black women is like Bitter-Sweet.

The Real Truth About
Black Men And Sex

CHAPTER 3

The Real Truth About
Black Men And Sex

Mythical beliefs and stereotypes about the Black Man's sexuality and his sexual appetite are having devastating effects on the Black Man's life. The following quote is an excerpt of a statement by Randall W. Maxey, M.D., Ph.D., from my book **Satisfying The Black Man Sexually Made Simple:**

> *"Society has inculcated both the Black Man and society in general,*

into the mythical belief that he, the Black Man, is a sexual animal or stud. When this normal, healthy man finds that he is (only) human in bed, it adds another failure to his already burden of feelings of inadequacy, resulting from social and economic insecurity. This results in difficult sexual relations which negatively impact all of his relationships with women. This self-fulfilling prophecy can create either dysfunction in sexuality or, at the very least, vastly unsatisfactory male-female relationships."

Performance anxiety (being the best and what it means): The Black Man is admonished to be the best in college, the best on the job, and society has placed the burden upon him to be the best in bed. The Black Man is constantly reminded that he must work three times harder and that he must be three times smarter than the White Man in order to be considered a competitor in the eyes of corporate America. The Black Man has been charged with the duty to be the best in bed; however, no other man has to wade through the bedroom with such a burden when he desires love, romance, and sex. Without a doubt, this **"performance anxiety"** causes sexual dysfunction. Sexual inadequacy is devastating to any man; it impacts his sexuality and his life in general.

Choosing partners in the bedroom: Sexual chaos and bedroom turmoil cause men to seek multiple sexual partners, cheat on their wives, (seeking to validate their sexual adequacy) become asexual, exhibit extreme irritation, and mood swings, develop low self-esteem and low self-worth, and to become very insecure. These sexual dilemmas often prompt Black Men into choosing White women as a means to validate their sexual worth and adequacy. Black men have bought into the notion that White women are less demanding, more sexually submissive, and have less sexual inhibitions than Black women. White women view oral sex as part of making love, and because she is more open to the usage of sexual toys, she becomes an ideal woman for a Black Man who is in need of a "Sexual Ego Boost." Sex is very important in one's life. Sexual activities have a strong influence on the way one thinks and performs in all areas of activity.

The value placed on sex: Besides money, sex is the only factor in our civilized societies that people contemplate at the risk of causing harm to themselves, or their families all for a few short hours of pleasure (if there is foreplay) and a few seconds of orgasmic thrills. It is the only factor that can cause a community-wide, a citywide, a national, or international calamity. Sex is a dominating factor in our lives, a moving force that keeps us going, as most of us will admit. Sex is a biological necessity that dominates us all in one way or another. Yet our society, which has made great scientific advancements, seeks to ignore it.

Men have lost their lives for **SEX**, lost their jobs for **SEX**, left their wives for **SEX,** left their children for **SEX**, left school for **SEX**, and have gone A.W.O.L. from the military for **SEX**. Yet, society continues **to "hold"** SEX a **"taboo."**

Male Impotency: The Black Man is at great risk of becoming sexually impotent due to the socioeconomic factors that impact his life. This causes damage to his physical and mental health, and therefore to his sexuality.

Foolish health choices, medications and their effects: The Black man is pressured by the feeling that he has to match up with the sexual script written for him by society. This pressure can lead him to cease taking medications prescribed for health conditions such as hypertension, etc., because they can cause impotency. Newer medications have overcome several of these problems. However, when confronted with a choice between the

"Heart" and the "Hard," many men choose the "Hard." For some men, their manhood and self-image is validated by this thing called "Penis." Many Black men have had heart attacks and suffered strokes because they quit taking their medications. It is sad when a man feels compelled to sacrifice his life, to leave his children without a father, to leave a spouse lonely and often financially devastated, for an erect penis.

Power or prowess: The Black Man has received world notoriety for his sexual prowess. You can ask anybody anywhere in the world what he/she knows about the Black Man, and he/she will not address his achievements, his inventions, his accomplishments, but instead will address his sexual prowess. Sexual prowess notoriety causes many Black men to view their penis as their most valuable asset and their source of power. Even today, the size of the Black man's penis and his sexual prowess is the focus of daily conversations. Many Black men are so obsessed with their penis size and sexual prowess that it causes him to jeopardize his life by refusing to take medications that impact his ability to obtain a long lasting erection.

The Black Man needs to develop a keener insight into and better understanding of his own sexuality. A woman cannot embrace the black man in a manner that is conducive to his total well being without understanding his sexuality, and how stereotypical mystical beliefs have impacted his life and, therefore, his sexuality.

It is very critical that the black community deal with sex straight-up and head-on in order to prevent our Black men from self-destruct-ion. It is also important for Black men to understand the power of herbs in treating sexual dysfunction. Many Black men are in such panic status that they are willing to place their lives in the hands of a surgeon for any little sexual issue. Remember, for many Black men, particularly those who are economically deprived, sexual gratification is the only form of gratification within their reach.

SEXUAL POTENCY

In The United States alone, at least 30 million older men have laboratory evidence of testosterone deficiency. Testosterone controls sexual energy, positive moods, physical strength, health of skin and hair, and a lot more. Women also depend on testosterone levels for sexual interest. Sperm formation in males is controlled entirely by testosterone levels. Therefore, inadequate sperm formation makes conception difficult or impossible.

A complicating factor in declining hormone levels is diminishing circulation, especially to the sexual apparatus. These two problems usually produce impotency in males. Ask the body to make more by offering testosterone simulating nutrients.

Stress, along with high levels of estrogen, can cause a lower level of testosterone in younger males. Older men tend to lack testosterone because of poor circulation and a natural decline of hormone secretion during later years. Clogged or blocked arteries can effect a man's ability to have an erection.

Poor circulation causes low testosterone levels, and is thus the number one cause for a decline in sexual interest in males. This lack of adequate circulation to the penis means an inability to produce an erection, but it doesn't necessarily mean a lack of desire.

The following information concerns sexual potency: This list of herbs has been used to treat sexual dysfunctions. You should see your doctor for a medical evaluation when experiencing sexual dysfunction.

Stif herbal Tonic - A vasodilator. It opens blood vessels, thereby improving circulation.

Arginine - A vasodilator. It opens blood vessels, especially the small ones, thereby, improving circulation.

Yohimbe - Causes enlargement of blood vessels and increased reflex excitability of the sacral region of the spinal cord. A wake-up call for a region of the body that may have gone to sleep. Decreases venous outflow from the penis, and increases arterial inflow, thus maximizing its effect.

* Ginkgo biloba - improves circulation.

* Red Clover and Nettles - Food for extra energy. They work well, and both are strong tonics. These two items have some aphrodisiacal qualities, also.

The Black Woman Before
Slavery

CHAPTER 4

The Black Woman
Before Slavery

According to history, the majority of Black people brought to America came from West African societies. It was during the late seventeenth, eighteenth, and early nineteenth centuries that Black African women were brought to America.

The Black Woman in Africa played roles that were vital to the survival of her people.

Her most important function was motherhood. She was highly visible in the economic market-place, controlling certain industries such as: sewing, selling cloth and pottery, and trading and selling goods of various kinds. She also had responsibility for raising food for her family by planting crops and attending to them. Because the Black Woman held a high economic position, many became independently wealthy.

The Black Woman took care of her children and prepared meals for her husband. She had less physical obligations with her husband because, more than likely, he had more then one wife.

The Black Woman's role as a mother took priority over her husband and the market-place. When she became pregnant, she would leave her husband's house and go to her father's house. She stayed there until her baby was weaned, usually for approximately three years. The same routine was repeated with each pregnancy. One can see clearly that the Black Woman lived as a independent woman with her children. The children went everywhere with the mother, tied to her back. The children were very close to their mothers. The strongest bond in slavery was that between mother and child.

The Black Woman felt very good about herself. There was no doubt about her being the essence of femininity and beauty. There was no measuring up to some one else's standard of beauty. The African Woman was the standard by which beauty was measured.

Many loving relationships have been ruined between the Black Woman and her man because of a lack of knowledge about the Black Woman's history.

The Effect Of Slavery On
The Black Woman's
Sexuality

CHAPTER 5

The Effects Of Slavery On The Black Woman's Sexuality

Did you know that the Black woman did not come to America on an airplane? She was thrown on the same slave ship as the Black man. The Black woman was exploited as a laborer in the fields. The Black woman was also exploited as a breeder, a domestic household worker, and as a sex object for the white man. The Black woman was also branded with a hot iron, and was beaten severely when she cried during the process. She was forced to take off

73

her clothing so she could be beaten on all parts of her body. The Black woman was forced to walk around naked as a constant reminder of her sexual vulnerability.

Bell Hooks, in her book, <u>Ain't I A Woman</u>, had the following to say regarding the Black woman's slave experience:

> *African females received the brunt of this mass brutalization and terrorization not only because they could be victimized via their sexuality but also because they were more likely to work intimately with the white family than the black male. Since the slaver regarded the black woman as a marketable cook, wet nurse, and housekeeper, it was crucial that she be so thoroughly terrorized that she would submit passively to the will of the white master, mistress, and their children. In order to make his product salable, the slaver had to ensure that no resistant black female would poison a family, kill children, set fire to the house, or resists in any way.*

The Black Woman was stripped of her dignity on every level. She was raped and beaten by White men and Black men alike. She was often used by White men for various selfish reasons such as:

*To increase the family size for the sole purpose of producing new slave hands.

*To take care of their children's physical and emotional needs (They were amazed at how the Black woman was able to modify their spoiled rotten children's behavior in a positive way by giving them love. The white children could feel the love that radiated from the Black woman. This is the reason they would run up to hug her when their parents were out of their sight, in spite of the low-down evil talk about Blacks they had heard from their parents and family members during open conversations.)

*To help work the cotton fields.

*To give him an earthly - heavenly experience when between her legs.

I once had a conversation with an old White man in Mississippi, who I met through my father; they were both farm owners. I remember asking him, specifically whether or not it was pure hatred for the Black woman that made White men rape her. I was shocked and astounded to find out that it was not pure hatred, but pure lust for the Black woman's beautiful body that led to such a violent act. He went on to describe how beautifully rounded the shape of her butt was, and how much pleasure and excitement he got from riding by in his truck, watching the Black woman bent over in the fields. Then he talked about how large their breasts were as they stood at attention like soldiers in the army. As I stood listening, I was totally amazed and overwhelmed as I thought -- "Wow! All this time, I thought they hated the very sight of the Black woman, but it was just the opposite." Nevertheless, the White's man's behavior was still demeaning.

In the fundamentalist Christian teaching, women were viewed as an evil sexual temptress. A White woman desiring sex was seen as a degraded and immoral human being. The White woman who suppressed her sexual feelings was looked upon as a goddess, innocent, pure, and holy.

Black women were viewed as sexually promiscuous savages. Since women were designated as the originator of sexual sin, the Black women were naturally seen as the embodiment of female evil and sexual lust. They were labeled Jezebels and sexually temptresses, and accused of leading White men away from spiritual purity into sin. One White politician urged that the Blacks be sent back to Africa so that White men would not fornicate and commit adultery. His words were "remove this temptation from us."

Since White women were not labeled sexually promiscuous savages; they do not come under scrutiny for their sexual appetites or behavior. Black women are always conscious of how they are viewed when it comes to their sensuality and sexuality. Black women are least likely to report rape, as a result of the sexually promiscuous stigma. Black men view White women as easier to get sexually because they do not play the games that Black women play. Black women tend to play hard-to-get as a result of the stigmas regarding their sexual behavior. The Black woman is least likely to be a sexual freak, because having a reputation for being moral and good is important to her. The Black woman who becomes an all-out-freak is a woman who is trying to compete with the White woman sexually in order to keep her Black man. As we approach the New Millennium, one hundred and thirty-three years past slavery, the Black woman is still haunted by the effects of slavery on her sexuality.

CHAPTER 6

The Black Woman In America

CHAPTER 6

The Black Woman In America

The stress imposed on the Black woman today has taken a toll on her life. The Black woman suffers more from racism and sexism than do women of other ethnic groups. Approximately 60% of current "heads" of household in the African-American community are women. She is the most frequent victim of rape and assault, and most of these crimes go unreported. There are many reasons for this. She may be afraid the authorities won't believe her. She may fear ostracism by fellow Blacks if she reports a Black person to the White man (the police). She is afraid to seek help and protection from the law because her black man might be overly punished, even killed, especially if he is outraged and has a high temper. A heavy burden rests upon the shoulders of the Black woman to protect the Black man at all costs.

A Black woman who divorces a financially empowered Black man, usually does not demand support for herself nor for her children if she has to go through the legal system.

The Black woman suffers abuse in her relationships with men, because she sees herself as his protector. This behavior is embedded in the Black woman's psyche. She has often seen her man beaten to the point of death in the presence of herself and her children. She has witnessed her man being sold away from her. She has witnessed her man leaving family behind and fleeing for his life after an altercation with a White man.

Women of all races want to feel a sense of independence. However, the Black woman has been forced to live and to be independent of her man ever since slavery.

Black women suffer more abuse on the job than Black males do. In many cases, she is the bread winner: therefore, she is afraid to report abuse, and afraid to quit the job. The result is a Black woman afraid to leave her job, no matter how abusive; and afraid to leave her man; no matter how abusive. She has been told that one-third of all Black men are either in jail or in the judicial system; one-third of all Black men are gay; and the last one-third want only White women. She becomes determined to stay with her man.

The media spotlights high-profile "Negroes" with White women, and fails to call attention to the many White women who take care of Black men financially; and the White women who are in relationships with Black men who are economically deprived.

Earl Ofari Hutchinson, Ph.D., in his book The Assassination of the Black Male Image, stated: "...*95% of Black men marry Black women.*" This may be true regarding marriages, however, there are a large number of Black men who have Common-law living arrangements, and a large number who date White women exclusively. This picture is not pretty for Black women staring at statistics such as 14% of White women never marry versus 35% of Black women who never marry."

Black women in America are struggling and battling with self-image, good hair, bad hair, skin too dark, skin too light, financial struggle, relationship struggle, loyal-to-the-Black-man struggle.

STRUGGLE, STRUGGLE, STRUGGLE!!!

Black male/female relationships are headed for trouble. There are several books on the market authored by Black men who are bashing Black women. These books can be dangerous to the credulous. One author stated the following: "Black men must form alliances and finally marry women from Africa, Asia, or Latin America." Where were these women when Ida B. Wells was on the front line fighting to end the lynching of Black men in the South? Where were these women when Black women were being raped, and their Black men were unable to defend them? Where were these women when Black men and Black women shared equal status as slaves? Where were they when Harriet Tubman was leading Black men and women to freedom land? When Madam C. J. Walker attended the National Negro Business League, and Booker T. Washington ignored her attempt to speak. Walker sprang to her feet and said, "Surely you are not going to shut the door in my face. I feel that I am in a business that is a credit to the womanhood of our race. I started in business seven years ago with only $1.50." And where were these women when Rosa Parks' aggressiveness, not passiveness but aggressiveness, changed the way Black men and women were being treated in America?

African-American women are often left to rear their children alone. Being alone is one of the Black woman's greatest fears. This fear is so overwhelming that the Black woman hesitates to express needs and wishes in her relationships.

Media propaganda is increasing the fear and excessive anxiety of Black women. The Black man's future is a major topic for discussion on television and talk shows and in newspapers. The Black woman is constantly reminded that her man is an endangered species. She is not told how many non-Black men are in jail, or how many are expected to be jailed or paroled.

Many Black women suffer from depression. Some symptoms of depression include excessive sleeping, lack of energy, poor concentration, and short attention span. Women taking depressant medications sometimes suffer a decline in sex drive and gain weight, adding to their already low self-esteem.

Many Black women are fearful because of their lack of economic empowerment. The Black woman continues to be the lowest paid of all groups in the employment sector. Providing for the basic needs of her family is a constant challenge.

Many Black women fear for their children's safety because violence and crime is at an all-time high in their communities. Many fear their children may become involved in drug selling because of the financial rewards. Many Black women find it very hard to be in a relaxed and peaceful state of mind.

It is a known fact that many Black women are single parents. Being single is a big problem by itself for some women-some, but not all. Some single women view being single as a tragedy.

The key to changing the African-American community is to restore, revive and heal the, Black woman. As has been said by the Elders, a nation can rise no higher than its women. The hand that rocks the cradle is the hand that can positively change the nation.

What's The Media Got To Do With It?

CHAPTER 7

What's The Media Got To Do With It?

The media has depicted Blacks as "fuckers" and not "lovers." How often do we see Blacks portrayed in movies as being romantic lovers or shown making love in a passionate manner?

The movies today do such an injustice to the Black woman. She is so devalued portrayed as a slut or prostitute; and called names such as bitch, whore, and even more degrading names. Even sitcoms portray Black women as being head-strong and difficult to get along with. She is always plotting or planning something tricky.

The following is a chart from a textbook
Understanding Human Sexuality:

The Interaction of Gender and Ethnicity:
Stereotypes of Males and Females
from Different Ethnic Groups

Anglo-American Males	Anglo–American Females
Intelligent	Attractive
Egotistical	Intelligent
Upper Class	Egotistical
Pleasant/Friendly	Pleasant/Friendly
Racist	Blond/light hair
Achievement Oriented	Sociable
African-American Males	African-American Females
Athletic	Speak loudly
Antagonistic	Dark Skin
Dark Skin	Antagonistic
Muscular appearance	Athletic
Criminal activities	Pleasant/friendly
Speak loudly	Unmannerly
	Sociable

The Interaction of Gender and Ethnicity:

Stereotypes of Males and Females

from Different Ethnic Groups

Asian-American Males	Asian American Females
Intelligent	Intelligent
Short	Speak softly
Achievement oriented	Pleasant/friendly
Speak softly	Short
Hard workers	
Mexican-American Males	Mexican-American Females
Lower class	Black/brown/dark hair
Hard workers	Attractive
Antagonistic	Pleasant/friendly
Dark skin	Dark skin
Noncollege education	Lower class
Pleasant/friendly	Overweight
Black/brown/dark hair	Baby makers
Ambitionless	Family oriented

Responses show a mixture of gender and ethnicity stereotyping. Remember all over the world people's perception of Blacks are derived from the pictures that the media portray.

If you were a man seeking a relationship with a female, after reading the above chart, which woman would you choose?

As you can clearly see, the media has a lot to do with how men view both Black women and White women.

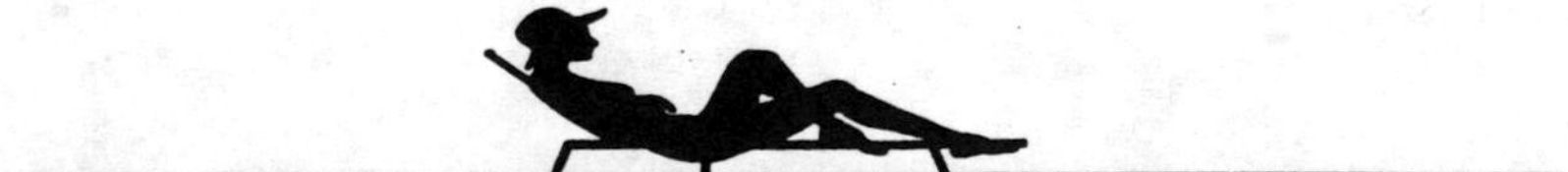

What's Music Got To Do
With It?

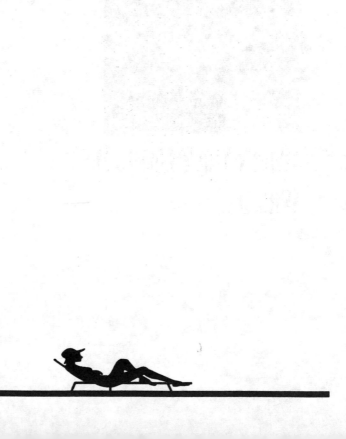

CHAPTER 8

What's Music Got To Do With It?

Some rap music conveys very positive messages, while other rap music conveys messages very detrimental to the image of the Black woman.

Young Black women are treated with much disrespect by young men today. After all, if you listen to music all day that refers to women as Bitches and Whores, you will internalize that perception of her. Your behavior toward her will be a reflection of your perception. Do men seek to love and have respect for Bitches and Whores and Rats? Many young Black men refer to young girls as rats. In fact, one of the common names for a young Black girl is Ho' referring to Whore.

The average Black girl is merely a sex object for the average young Black male. As he becomes aroused via his erotic music, he looks for easy prey. After satisfying his sexual lust, the Black girl is no more to him than his baby's mother.

Many artists sing about the Black woman as a gold-digger. The young Black man who is determined not to be a sucker (as they call it) will see to it that the only thing the young Black girl will get from him is a stiff penis, alcohol, and drugs.

Young men and young women will become adults and unfortunately their perception of each other will remain unchanged. He is a dog and she, the Black woman, is still perceived as the bitch and the whore.

Now who is viewed as "The Woman," "The Goddess?" It certainly is not the Black woman. What does rap music have to do with it? Judge for yourself.

WHY BLACK MEN CHOOSE WHITE WOMEN

CHAPTER 9

Why Black Men Choose
White Women

CHAPTER 9

Why Black Men Choose
White Women

I want to make it understood that I am not against interracial marriages. Everyone should have the right to choose his or her own soul mate. This chapter is designed to examine the reasons why Black men are choosing White women. According to the U.S. Census Bureau, one out of every 20 marriages is interracial. There were 246,000 Blacks married to Whites in this country last year, almost four times the number in 1970. According to statistics, the number of Black men that are married to White women far out-number any and all other cross-culture marriages.

Given the fact that approximately 60% of African Americans homes are headed by a female, (according to the U.S. census report) the decrease in the numbers of available African-American men, as well as the number of well educated and beautiful African American women, it seems to be about time that we examine the reasons why Black men are increasingly seeking White women.

Why do some Black men choose White women? The White woman, for years, has been portrayed as the very essence of beauty and the epitome of all that is good. She is portrayed in movies, magazines, and advertising commercials as a sex symbol. The White woman's breasts, her nearly nude body, and her wiggling butt are used to sell the beauty and value of the product.

America has done a great job of selling the White woman; it is not just the Black man who feels his self-esteem heightened by having her. However, this book addresses the Black man.

Many Black men have never witnessed romance between their mother and father. In fact, many of them do not see their fathers. Their orientation to hot juicy dripping romance is what they see in the movies or on T.V. between the White male and the White female. Their normal and natural responses were to lust for such juicy encounters with the White woman.

The Black woman has been portrayed very negatively in the movies. Only recently have you seen her passionately making love. You have seen her being raped, being abused, or offering to perform oral sex for drugs. You read about the Black welfare queens, the ones that are on the county, those who have babies and are not married, and how many of them will never be married. The Black woman has been given such titles as gold diggers, sapphires, male basher, and bitch. She has also been labeled as both domineering and sexually inhibited.

Stories are told about judges taking the Black man to the cleaners during a divorce from a Black woman. It is not widely publicized how much the White woman gets when she divorces the Black man.

Andrew Billingsley, Ph.D. in his book <u>Climbing Jacob's Ladder</u> had the following to say:

> *"The preponderance of African American men and White women in interracial marriages produced a theoretical explanation of interracial marriages Developed in 1941 by Robert Merton and Kingsley Davis, and supported by Robert Staples, this theory holds that African-American men are attracted to White women because*

their white caste status elevates the
Black partner's sense of importance."

Why else do Black men cross the racial line? Scholars suggest that Black girls maybe socialized by their mothers differently than Black boys. I would tend to agree. Black women remember mostly the pain associated with White men during slavery. The pain of abuse and rape. Many were raped at the early age of 13 years old. The Black man was raped also by the White woman; it provoked no physical pain but psychological damage was done. Many of them enjoyed the sex they had with the White woman because they saw it as a way of getting back at Mr. Charlie for having sex with their wives.

Many Black men were encouraged as boys by their fathers and friends to "get you some white pussy, man." I remember hearing men who lived in the South asking men who visited the North, "man, did you get you some white pussy?"

A Black man like any other man, wants the best that life has to offer, and for many Black men that means having a White woman. The best looking by European standards. The best sex – as they have seen in pornographic movies and magazines for years. A pushover - the White woman is said to be very submissive to the Black man. Some believe that the White woman may be submissive to the Black man because he treats her the way that she has been portrayed, as a precious stone, a royal queen, and Virgin Mary (once she gets out of bed).

An article by Susan Crain Bakos untitled "What are These Men Afraid Of (Sexually)?" in the January 1994 issue of *New Woman* stated the following:

> *"Number one on the average man's sexual wish list is more fellatio. They love the physical sensations, the complete attention being lavishing upon the penis, and even the feeling of being*

erotically under your power. Yes, they want more fellatio, but they also want their woman to get pleasure from performing it. You probably feel the same way about cunnilingus; you want it, but not from a man who is secretly thinking. 'Oh, Yuck!' as he does it."

I reiterate that all men share the desire for fellatio. Oral sex has been considered for Whites only. For years they were the only ones seen performing it in pornography movies and in pornography magazines.

During my research, I discovered that many Black men deny oral sex involvement. Don Spears says <u>In Search of GOODPUSSY.</u>

"There are several reasons why most Black men still deny that they perform oral sex on women. The most obvious reason is that some Black men really do not do it, and they probably never will. One of the reasons why those who do continue to say that they do not, however, is that they see oral sex as a

"A White Man's Thing." In fact, they know Black people in general believe anything that is not normal is something that sick White people do.

Another reason for denial is that many Black people tend to be moralistic and any sex act that is not missionary is wrong. Doing it any way but the right way is nasty."

During my survey, many Black men shared with me the following information: "Most Black women that performed fellatio did so only to please their men." They stated that they had to request it from the Black woman, whereas with the White woman it was a natural component of making love.

I remember the times when the most degrading and humiliating and inhumane words that Blacks could say to each other were "you suck my pussy" or "you suck my dick" or to call one a cocksucker. That was like talking about one's mother. Those were fighting words, not love and romance words.

Andrew Billingsley, Ph.D stated in <u>Climbing Jacob's Ladder</u>:

> *"These scholars point to the differential bases on which men and women select their mates. Women give greater weight to such factors as earning capacity and ambition. Men, on the other hand, are more likely to choose their mates on the bases of physical attraction. This suggests that in contemporary American society, White women are more likely to find Black men who meet their potential earning criteria than White men are to find Black women who meet their European conceptions of physical attractiveness. Conversely, Black men many of whom have internalized the same European conception of physical attractiveness are more likely to find White women who meet their criteria."*

Dr. Mack B. Morant had the following to say:

"Black men choose White women because they themselves are insane, miseducated, unconscious, and self haters."

I like the way Dr. Mack B. Morant explains the reasons for the insanity in his book <u>The Insane Nigger:</u>

"Having complete control over Africa, the colonial powers in Europe projected the images of Africa negatively. They always project Africa in a negative light: jungle savages, cannibals, nothing civilized. Why then naturally it was so negative to you and me, and you and I began to hate it. We didn't want anybody telling us anything about Africa, much less calling us Africans. In hating Africa and in hating Africans, we ended up hating ourselves, without even realizing it. Because you can't hate the roots of a tree, and not hate the tree. You can't hate your origin and not hate yourself. So they

*very skillfully make you and me hate
our African identity, our African char-
acteristics.*

*You know yourself that we have
been a people who hated our char-
acteristics. We hated our heads, the
shape of our nose, we wanted one of
those long dog like noses, you know;
we hated the color of our skin, hated
the blood of Africa that was in our
veins. And in hating our features
and our skin and our blood, why we
had to end up hating ourselves. And
we hated ourselves. Our color became
to us like a prison which we felt was
keeping us confined, not letting us go
this way or that way. We felt all of
these restrictions were based solely
upon our color, and the psychological reaction to that would have to be
that as long as we felt imprisoned or
chained or trapped by Black sin, Black
features and that blood holding us
back automatically had to become hateful to us. And it became hateful to
us. It made us feel inferior, it made us*

feel inadequate, made us feel helpless, and when we fell victims to this feeling of inadequacy or inferiority or helplessness, we turned to somebody else to show us the way.

The above passage gives you a vivid picture of how the Black man was made to hate his African heritage and his physical body. When one hates self, he or she is definitely insane. "When a person hates himself he is insane, his Black woman is an extension of himself, therefore, he cannot love her. It is a natural order for a person to want the best things in life. The best thing life has to offer as depicted by the White man is a White woman. He brutally fucked the Black man's woman in the presence of the Black man and his children, diminishing every ounce of pride the Black man held on to. I do not enjoy using profanity; however, I use 'fuck' because making love is a sharing and caring experience. He made the Black man believe that the White woman was untouchable, a

*sacred beauty that no man could ven-
ture into except a White man. His
"beautiful" White woman was left
home only to be admired; while he
got his sexual satisfaction from the
Black man's woman."*

I was told by the elders that when the White man entered a Black man's cabin, the Black man was made to leave the cabin or was made to stay and watch. I was told that when the White man finished he would pat the Black man on the head while leaving and the Black man would say "Massa, I hope you liked it." The White man would respond, "Yes, good pussy boy," as he went home to his sleeping beauty.

It was common knowledge which Black women were the White man's mistresses. The relationship between White men and Black women were the major factors in creating the brain damage the Black man has today for the White woman. When any individual is kept away from something for a long period of time by threats, he becomes curious.

Many black men who fought hard in the Civil Rights Movement were more interested in being able to have the White woman than in going to school together, eating together or riding the bus together.

A well know Black man gives this analysis. There is no love left between a Black man and a Black woman. Take me for instance, I love White women and hate Black women. It's just in me, so deep that I don't even try to get it out of me anymore. I'd jump over ten Nigger bitches just to get to a White woman. A white woman is beautiful even if she's bald headed and only has one tooth. It's just the fact that she's got smooth, white skin. I like to lick her White skin as it's sweet, fresh honey flows from her pores, and just touch her long soft, silky hair. There's softness about a White woman, something delicate and soft inside her.

But a Nigger bitch seems to be full of steel, granite hard and resisting, not soft and submissive like a White woman. Ain't nothing more beautiful than a White woman's hair being blown in the wind. The White woman is more than a woman to me... she's like a goddess, a symbol. My love for her is religious and beyond fulfillment. I worship her. I love a White woman's dirty drawers. Sometimes I think that the way I feel about White women, I must have gotten from my father and his father's father as far back as you go into slavery.

Black men who get married to White women are also trying to satisfy sociopsychological insanity from which they suffer in America. For example, this was the response of a Black man from Mississippi when he was asked why he married his White wife.

"What did I like best about Carol?
That she was hard to get. Her being
White had a lot to do with it. The
idea I wasn't supposed to have a White

*woman. After I knew that everyone
was going to be against it, I thought,
well if I'm successful, I will be the first
to do it. But actually it wasn't all
that. It's legal now, but I believe I
would have done it anyway. It wasn't
because I wanted to make a big bang
out of it. I really married her because I loved her. I would say the
White woman is much better than the
Black woman."*

Some of the reasons given by Black men
who date White women are: "When I am with
a White woman I feel like a man" (Remember,
society has labeled the Black woman strong
and the Black man weak; therefore he feels
strong with a White woman). "Also it gives me
great pleasure for the White man to see me
with his woman – the forbidden fruit."

Another reason Black men choose White
women is that White women are all but molest-
ing Black men. They are pulling after the Black
man as though he is the only man left on earth.

The White woman has heard so much about the Black man's sexuality, such as the "Mandingo," "Long John," full of energy, ever ready and long endurance. Therefore, she now aggressively seeks him. She has been denied the opportunity to enjoy a Black man, while the White man has enjoyed the Black woman.

The most critical reason Black men choose White women is because they continue to measure Black women by the European belief and value system. They view the Black woman as an Ebony Caucasian. Black men have not been stimulated nor motivated to fully under-stand the Black woman and to examine her unique past and present experiences that cause her behavior and sensitivity to be unique.

Shahrazad Ali in her book, <u>The Black Man's Guide to Understanding the Black Woman</u>, has the following to say:

> *The Black woman sees the Black man integrating too. She witnesses him dating and marrying the White woman so she considers her part of the*

contribution to the 50,000 Black women who date and marry White men as a small significance. While others of them complain that the Black man is with the White woman because she is easier to get along with, or that she gives him better sex, or that she respects him more. She doesn't know that he is with her for one reason only, he is with her because she gives him peace.

However, it is described, the end result he sees for himself is peace. Of course there are few who claim they are with the White woman because they are getting back at the White man or that they want to possess her because they were denied her. These are all flimsy and flaky excuses for not being familiar with the word peace. Certainly not all cases are the same."

Earl Ofari Hutchinson, Ph.D. explains the following about Black men and White women:

Ninety-five percent of Black men marry

Black women. Most of the guys that marry White women don't do it because they think these women are Green Goddess, forbidden fruit or possess mythical status. Nor do they marry them because they are lustful or filled with selfhate. They marry them for the same reason Black men marry Black women. They share common interests, and they love them. Every Black woman worried sick that all Black men want White women should take this test. Think of all the Black men you know. Now how many of them exclusively pursue, date, are married to or spend every working moment chattering about White women? Don't cheat.

Many reasons have been given as to why Black men choose White women. I have heard and read reasons as simple as opposites attract. The Black man wants to get revenge. It is God's way of bringing all people together. I believe that after reading this entire book, you will truly understand the Black man's re-

relationship with the Black Woman and why he chooses the White woman.

CHAPTER 10

Are Black Women
GoldDiggers?

CHAPTER 10

ARE BLACK WOMEN GOLDDIGGERS?

I find it quite interesting that the Black minority always represents the majority when it comes to Black issues. Are most Black women more materialistic than other women? And do most Black women keep their hands in their men's wallets? Is there any truth to the saying that Black women ask more of their men?

If there is any truth to the old saying, could it be that, Black women ask for more because they have so much less than other women? And if Black women were truly "Gold Diggers," most of them would not talk to Black men. After all, how many Black men have Gold (Deep pockets) in America?

The White woman is viewed as the Goddess; therefore she is to have the best without asking. The Black man will give freely to the White woman the things that a Black woman would have to ask for.

I interviewed the family members of men who choose White women. The majority of them shared with me that these men treated the White women much better than they did the Black women in their lives. They further stated that the family member treated the White in-laws better than the Black in-laws. I conclude that you give to the Goddess before she asks. You anticipate her needs and desires. She expects to be treated in such fashion.

On television, she is seen living in a nice home, driving a nice car, wearing nice clothes and jewelry. Black men have internalized that media perception of the White woman. Most

Black men do not live next door to White women, they do not go to school with them, they do not socialize with them. Their perception and their reality of White women are filtered through the eyes of the media.

In order for us to understand this money issue and materialistic issues, we must examine our slave history in America. I realize that many Blacks want to go forward and never look back; however, we must reflect on our past in order to gain a better perspective of our present behavior and attitude.

Black women were socialized during their slave experience to barter or trade sex for money, things, and favors. The Black woman who slept with the White man without resisting him and who was at his beck and call, was given money, clothes and favor. It was common knowledge among Blacks as to which women were sleeping with Mr. Charlie. It was like a silent code, because no one ever talked about it. The sexual bartering between White men and Black women was the means of putting enough food on the table for herself, her man, and her children. The White woman and the White wives knew what was happening, but could do nothing about it. The White woman learned the trade of sexual bartering from the Black slave woman. Today as I write, White women are sexing their way to the top of Corporate America. They learned from observing the White man and the Black slave woman what White men will do for a "little piece of real estate with grass growing on it" (called pussy). Most slaves who were brought from Africa settled in the South. Many young Black girls had babies as a result of being raped by their white master or overseer. These men continued business as usual, raping the same girl again or other girls, leaving their seeds behind without recognition or acknowledgment.

If this page looks a little wet, then forgive me because I am crying as I write. My soul aches, my whole body hurts, the pain of my ancestors flows through my veins as I embark upon telling this untold story. I wish I could end this chapter here, but I cannot. The young Black girls were left with babies, without means to provide for them. Here I am crying again. Oh, the thought of a mother and father whose daughter is pregnant by a White man and they cannot do a thing about it. Okay, I am back to writing. I have dried the tears – to cry no more soon, okay.

The mother and father of the young teen provided shelter and food for the teen mother and her child. If the teen mother wanted nice clothes for herself and her child she had to barter for it. What did she have to trade? She owned nothing, except her tender body.

Growing up in Mississippi. I witnessed women in my family -- decent women -- who had sex with married men, not for love but for money, for a new dress, a new pair of shoes for herself or for her baby. They wanted things that their parents could not buy for them. Black men, as well as White men, took advantage of the economic need of these hurting

Black women. There were no jobs for the average young woman in the South other than seasonal farming; in between farming season there was not much to do. Kids who did not have babies went to school during those times. Girls who had babies were not allowed to mix with the girls who did not have babies; therefore she could not return to school (can you believe that?). One more tears for me.

This young woman is now at the mercy of others in every way. What does she have to offer? Young men her age have nothing to offer her. And after all they are told not to marry a woman with a child (a ready-made family they called it). Has anything changed? Black women continue to be at the bottom of the economic pole. Today, Black teens find themselves following in the foot-steps of their mothers. They see the favors their mothers receive from their men. They hear their mothers talking about what their men bought for them. Remember, children learn what they see.

Teen girls miss the precious opportunity to enjoy the puppy-love experience shared between teenagers. Unfortunately, many Black teens come from economically deprived homes; therefore, they seek relationships with older men who can buy them things, pick them up from school and take them places in their nice automobiles. They give these men sex in exchange for money, things, and a ride in his car.

Now what do you have? Young men with a bad attitude and bad perceptions of Black women. A Black woman becomes, in the eyes of the young Black man, a whore because the older men are buying sex from her. The young Black male cannot compete with the 24-29-year-old men who prey on these young girls, unless he is the young Black man who resorts to selling drugs or some other illegal activities. The young Black male then becomes angry with the teenage girl, not with the older Black male. To him she is a whore, a bitch and a low down gold digging rat. Does his perception of her change as he gets older? The answer is no. Because the young girl who was dating the older male is now left behind with a child or two, she has low self-esteem. She is angry and she comes with more baggage than most Black men are willing or capable of dealing with. Her financial needs are great, and the average Black man can barely support himself and the babies he has fathered outside of marriage.

With the historical and present facts before you, what is your conclusion? Are Black women "Golddiggers," or are they just in a bad economic situation? I do believe that men who view Black women as "Golddiggers" are men who have only been in relationships with economically deprived women. Women who are economically empowered only ask from men love, respect, and time.

Let us learn the facts and get rid of myths that are hurting and destroying Black male/ female relationships.

CONCLUSION

CONCLUSION

I conclude that I have laid the facts before you. As a mother offers her breasts to her baby, as a wife who prepares the food and sets the table for her husband, as the farmer prepares and leaves food out for his animals, you have what you need. That is THE TRUTH. You can eat and live or you can starve and die. Remember, the Elders have warned us before that the Truth Shall Make You Free. When we become free, then our children and our children's children will be free.

Bibliography

Bibliography

Ali, Shahrazad. *The Blackman's Guide to Understanding The Black-woman.* Philadelphia: Civilized Publication, 1990.

Bakos, SusanCrain.*"What Are These Men Afraid Of (Sexually)?"* New Woman Magazine, January 1994

Billingsley, Ph.D., Andrew. *Climbing Jacob's Ladder: The Enduring Legacy of African American Families.* New York: Simon & Schuster, 1992.

Hooks, Bell. *Ain't I A Woman,* South End Press, 1981

Cornish, Gracie, Ph.D., *Radiant Women of Color,* Kola Publishing N.Y., N.Y. 1994

Hutchinson, Ph.D., Earl Ofari. *The Assassination of The Black Male Image.* Los Angeles: Middle Passage Press, 1994.

King, Victoria, *Manhandled.* Memphis: Derek Winston, 1992.

McQueen, William. *The X-Rated Sex Book.* Lake Hiawatha: Margrevar, Inc., 1992

Millligan, Ph.D., Rosie. *Satisfying The Black Woman Sexually Made Simple.* Los Angeles: Professional Business Consultants, 1990.

Millligan, Ph.D., Rosie. *Satisfying The Black Man Sexually Made Simple.* Los Angeles: Professional Business Consultants, 1994.

Millligan, Ph.D., Rosie. *Nigger, Please.* Los Angeles: Professional Business Consultants, 1996.

Morant, Dr, Mack. *The Insane Nigger.* Holly Hill: R&M Publishing Co., 1978.

Bibliography

Spears, Don. *In Search of GOODPUSSY: Living Without Love The Real Truth About Men and Their Relationships.* New Orleans: Don Spears, 1992

Welsing, Dr. Frances Cress. *The Isis Paper.* Chicago: Third World Press, 1989.

Winfield, Sidney. *Positive African-American Men United.* Nashville TN. 1997

Janet Shibley Hyde/John Delamater, *Understanding Human Sexuality.* Mcgraw-Hill New York. Published Date 1994 Copyright Date 1997.